The Caitlin Clark Story:
Inspiring Tales Of An Unstoppable Rising Star.

By

David Grant

Table of Content

Career highlights and awards

Introduction

Early Life

High School Career

College Career

National Team Career

Player Profile

Off The Court

Conclusion

Career highlights and awards

AP Player of the Year (2023)
Naismith College Player of the Year (2023)
USBWA National Player of the Year (2023)
Wade Trophy (2023)
2× Unanimous first-team All-American (2022, 2023)
2× First-team All-American – AP (2022, 2023)
3× First-team All-American – USBWA (2021–2023)
3× WBCA Coaches' All-American (2021–2023)

Second-team All-American – AP (2021)

3× Dawn Staley Award (2021-2023)

2× Nancy Lieberman Award (2022, 2023)

USBWA National Co-Freshman of the Year (2021)

WBCA Co-Freshman of the Year (2021)

2× Big Ten Player of the Year (2022, 2023)

3× First-team All-Big Ten (2021–2023)

Big Ten Freshman of the Year (2021)

her debut season. In her second season, Clark led Division I in both points and assists for the first time ever, earning her a spot on the first team of All-Americans by receiving a unanimous vote. As a junior, she received the national player of the year award and was once more chosen for the first team of All-Americans. She has received the Dawn Staley Award twice and the Nancy Lieberman Award once for being the top Division I player in her position.

Clark has brought home three gold medals for the United States at the youth international level. She was chosen as the Most Valuable Player in the FIBA Under-19 Women's Basketball World Cup in 2021.

Early Life

Brent Clark and Anne Nizzi-Clark welcomed Clark into the world on January 22, 2002 in Des Moines, Iowa. Her mother is of Italian descent. Clark's father played basketball and baseball at Simpson College. Her housemates while growing up in West Des Moines, Iowa, were Colin, a younger brother, and Blake, an older brother who is presently playing college football for Iowa State.

When Clark started playing basketball at age five, she was the only girl on a boys' youth team. She played softball, volleyball, soccer, and tennis as a kid before focusing on basketball.

In the sixth grade, Clark started playing basketball for the All Iowa Attack of Ames, Iowa, and she did so all the way through high school. She was up against high school seniors by the seventh grade. The Minnesota Lynx are the closest WNBA club to Clark's hometown, and after being motivated by their star player Maya Moore, she traveled with her father on a 3-and-a-half-hour drive to watch them play. She also looked up to her cousins Haley and Audrey Faber, who played basketball for Dowling Catholic High School in West Des Moines, as well as Harrison Barnes, a former All-Iowa Attack player.

High School Career

Clark played four seasons of varsity basketball at Dowling Catholic High School for head coach Kristin Meyer. As a freshman, she averaged 15.3 points, 4.7 assists, and 2.3 steals per game while being chosen to the Class 5A All-State second team. She also helped her team get to the state quarterfinals. During her sophomore season, Clark averaged 27.1 points, 6.5 rebounds, four assists, and 2.3 steals, helping Dowling Catholic finish 20-4 and go to the state semifinals. She placed second in the state in scoring and was chosen for the Class 5A All-State first team.

In a 90-78 victory over Mason City High School on February 4, 2019, Clark—then a junior—had the second-best five-on-five scoring performance in Iowa history with 60 points. She broke the state single-game record with her 13 three-pointers made throughout the game. Clark's final season statistics were a state-best 32.6 points, 6.8 rebounds, 3.6 assists, and 2.3 steals per game. Her leadership helped Dowling Catholic reach the state playoffs and a 17-8 overall record. Clark was selected for the Class 5A All-State first team and won the Iowa Gatorade Player of the Year award. As a senior, she once again led the state in scoring with an average of 33.4 points, 8 rebounds, 4 assists, and 2.7

steals per game. Her team finished the season with a record of 19-4 and progressed to the Class 5A regional final before falling to Sioux City East High School. At the conclusion of her career, Clark had 2,547 points, placing her fourth all-time in Iowa five-on-five scoring. She was recognized as the Iowa Gatorade Player of the Year, the Des Moines Register All-Iowa Athlete of the Year, and Iowa Miss Basketball in addition to being named to the Class 5A All-State first team.

Both the McDonald's All-American Game and the Jordan Brand Classic, where Clark had been selected to play, had to be canceled because of the COVID-19 outbreak.

In high school, Clark played AAU basketball with future Iowa State athletes Ashley and Aubrey Joens for All Iowa Attack. She helped the team finish second in 2017 and 2018 and win the Nike Elite Youth Basketball League championship in 2018. For her first two years at Dowling Catholic, Clark started playing varsity soccer, but then moved to basketball for her final two.

College Career

Freshman season

In her first season, Clark started at point guard for Iowa. On November 25, 2020, she made her collegiate debut in a 96-81 victory over Northern Iowa, tallying 27 points, eight rebounds, and four assists. In her second game on December 2, Clark defeated Drake 103-97 with 30 points and 13 assists to earn her first double-double. She accomplished the feat on

December 22 in a 92-65 victory over Western Illinois, the first triple-double by an Iowa player since Samantha Logic did it in 2015. On just 3-of-15 field goal attempts, Clark finished the game with 13 points, 13 rebounds, and 10 assists. On January 6, 2021, she contributed 37 points, 11 rebounds, and 4 assists in a 92-79 victory over Minnesota. On February 11, Clark scored a season-high 39 points, 10 rebounds, and seven assists in an 88-81 victory over Nebraska, shattering the

Pinnacle Bank Arena single-game scoring record for Nebraska. On February 28, she defeated Wisconsin 84–70 with 18 points and a season-high 14 assists. Clark was chosen as the unquestioned Big Ten Freshman of the Year and a member of the first team All-Big Ten at the completion of the regular season. By receiving the Big Ten Freshman of the Week award 13 times, she established a conference record. She also held the most Player of the

Week accolades in the Big Ten with five.

Clark helped Iowa to a runner-up finish at the Big Ten tournament, where she was chosen for the all-tournament team and had the most assists ever (37). In the NCAA tournament's second round victory over Kentucky, she provided 35 points, seven rebounds, and six assists. She broke program single-game records for points and three-pointers during the competition (six). Even though

Iowa made it to the Sweet 16 with to Clark's 21 points, they fell to top-seeded UConn 92-72. She was also selected for the first team of the United States Basketball Writers Association (USBWA), the second team of the Associated Press (AP), and the Women's Basketball Coaches Association (WBCA) Coaches' All-America team. Clark became the first freshman to receive the Dawn Staley Award, which is given to the best guard in Division I. She and UConn's Paige Bueckers shared the Tamika Catchings Trophy and the WBCA Freshman of the Year Award, two prestigious Division I honors. As a rookie, Clark averaged 26.6 points, 7.1 assists, and 5.9 rebounds per game. She led the NCAA Division I in scoring and was second in both assists and three-pointers made per game. She had the fourth-highest scoring average in Iowa history and set freshman program records for points and assists. She also led Division I in points, assists, field goals, and three-pointers.

Sophomore season

On November 9, 2021, Clark defeated New Hampshire 93-50 in her sophomore season debut while recording 26 points, 8 rebounds, and 6 assists. On January 2, 2022, she defeated Evansville 93-56 while scoring 44 points and handing out eight assists. Clark beat Ohio State's Kelsey Mitchell to become the fastest Big Ten player to 1,000 career points. She also broke the women's single-game scoring record at Carver-Hawkeye

Arena. On January 16, 2022, she recorded her fourth triple-double of the year while leading her team to a 93-83 victory over Nebraska with 31 points, 10 rebounds, and 10 assists. Four days later, Clark defeated Minnesota 105-49 in her subsequent game with 35 points, 13 rebounds, and 11 assists. She accomplished consecutive triple-doubles with at least 30 points for the first time ever by a men's or women's player in Division I history, and she was the first woman to do so in Big Ten history. With 20 points, seven rebounds, and 18 assists on January 25, Clark defeated Penn State 107-79, setting a single-game record for the program and the conference. On January 31, she contributed 43 points, seven assists, and four rebounds in a 92-88 loss against Ohio State. On February 6, Michigan defeated the team 98-90 despite Clark scoring a career-high 46 points, including 25 in the fourth quarter, and dishing out 10 assists. She surpassed the female single-game scoring record in the Crisler Center, the home of Michigan. After helping Iowa capture a share of the regular season championship, she was chosen by the Big Ten coaches and media as the league's Player of the Year and first-team All-Big Ten.

On March 5, 2022, Clark scored 83 points while grabbing 66 rebounds against Nebraska in the Big Ten tournament semifinals. She contributed to Iowa winning the championship and was chosen as the game's most outstanding player (MOP). Her team lost to Creighton in the second round of the NCAA tournament 64-62, and Clark was held to a season-low 15 points and 11 assists on 4-of-19 shooting from the field. Along with being named to the first team of All-Americans by the AP and USBWA, she was also chosen for the WBCA Coaches' All-America Team. She received unanimous first-team All-American recognition. As the best Division I point guard,

Clark won the Nancy Lieberman Award and the Dawn Staley Award for the first time in history. She had a game average of 27 points, 8 rebounds, and 8 assists as a sophomore. In a single season, Clark became the first woman to top Division I in both points scored and assists provided. She also held the Division I record for triple-doubles, free throws, and overall points.

Junior season

Clark was chosen unanimously for the AP preseason All-America team entering her junior season, and the Big Ten coaches and media chose her as the league's preseason player of the year. On November 18, 2022, she lost to Kansas State 84-83 with 27 points, 10 rebounds, and 7 assists before suffering an ankle injury with 3.8 seconds left. When Iowa faced Belmont on November 20, Clark's status was classified as day-to-day. In the 73-62 triumph for the Hawkeyes, he scored 33 points. In a 94-81 loss to NC State on December 1, she scored a season-high 45 points. With 22 points, 10 rebounds, and 10 assists three days later in a 102-71 victory over Wisconsin, Clark recorded her ninth triple-double of her career. She defeated Samantha Logic to take the Big Ten lead in triple-doubles. On December 21, in her 75th game, Clark tied Delaware's Elena Delle Donne for the fastest Division I women's player reach 2,000 career points since the 1999-2000 season by scoring 20 points in a 92-54 victory over Dartmouth. On January 23, 2023, with 28 points, 15 assists, and 10 rebounds, Clark defeated the previously unbeaten AP No. 2 Ohio State team 83-72. She had 42 points, 8 assists, and 7 rebounds in a 96-82 victory over Maryland on February 2. On February 26, Clark had 34 points, nine rebounds, nine assists, and the game-winning three-pointer at the buzzer to lead the team to an 86-85 victory over AP No. 2 Indiana. At the end of the regular season, she received a unanimous vote for the Big Ten Player of the Year award once more, and the league's coaches and media chose her for the Big Ten's first team.

For guiding Iowa to its second straight victory in the Big Ten Tournament, Clark was honored with MOP accolades. When she defeated Ohio State 105-72 in the tournament's championship game with 30 points, 17 assists, and 10 rebounds, she became the first player to achieve a triple-double. With her tenth triple-double, Clark moved up to second place in Division I history, passing Sabrina Ionescu. In the Elite Eight of the NCAA tournament, she defeated Louisville 97-83 with 41 points, 12 assists, and 10 rebounds. She accomplished a triple-double of 30 or 40 points, becoming the first player in men's or women's tournament history to do so. Clark made history by being the first player in Division I to finish a season with at least 900 points and 300 assists. Clark's effort earned her the title of Seattle 4 Regional MOP, and as a result, Iowa advanced to its first Final Four since 1993. She helped her team defeat the defending champion and unbeaten South Carolina by a score of 77-73 in the Final Four, snapping their 42-game winning streak. She finished with 41 points, eight assists, and six rebounds. She became the first participant in the history of the event to have back-to-back 40-point games and broke the semifinals women's tournament single-game scoring record. Following their victory, Iowa advanced to their first participation in a championship game in women's basketball program history.

The Wade Award, the Naismith College Player of the Year, the USBWA National Player of the Year, and the AP Player of the Year awards went to Clark. She received first-team honors from the AP and USBWA and was named to the WBCA Coaches' All-America Team. She was a unanimous first-team All-American for the second season in a row.

National team career

Clark competed for the United States in the 2017 FIBA Under-16 Women's Americas Championship in Buenos Aires, Argentina. She was a backup who averaged 8.8 points per game while guiding her side to a perfect 5-0 record and the gold medal. Clark took part in the 2019 FIBA Under-19 Women's Basketball World Cup in Bangkok, Thailand. In her seven games, she averaged 5.3 points, helping her team win another gold medal with a perfect 7-0 record. At Debrecen, Hungary in 2021, Clark assisted the United States in taking home the gold medal in the FIBA Under-19 Women's Basketball World Cup. She averaged a team-high 14.3 points, 5.6 assists, and 5.3 rebounds per game and was named the Most

Valuable Player and to the All-Tournament Team.

Player profile

Clark, a point guard, is an excellent height for the position at 6 feet 0 inches (1.83 m). She is a proficient scorer who has the range to make baskets from up close, midrange, and beyond the arc. Clark has incredible range, frequently and difficultly shooting from a significant distance behind the three-point line. She has been likened to shooters in the National Basketball Association (NBA) like Trae

Young, Damian Lillard, and Stephen Curry. Clark is a gifted playmaker who can find her teammates in defensive swarms and pass in front in transition. Because of her ability to pass and score, she excels in pick-and-roll situations. Clark has been compared to Diana Taurasi in terms of talent and personality. Coach Lisa Bluder of Iowa compared her to Sabrina Ionescu and Sue Bird.

Off the court

One of the most financially viable college basketball players, according to analysts, is Clark. On August 18, 2021, she signed a NIL (first name, image, and likeness) deal with the Vinyl Studio in West Des Moines, Iowa. On October 27, she signed a contract with the enormous grocery chain Hy-Vee. On March 1, 2022, H&R Block officially announced Clark as a participant in its "A Fair Shot" program to support female college sports. On July 26, she inked a NIL contract with Topps, launching trading cards for college athletes. Before the start of her junior year at Iowa, Clark signed a deal with Nike. During the 2023 NCAA tournament, she was one of five women's college basketball players highlighted by Buick's "See Her Greatness" campaign, which attempted to raise the visibility of women in sports.

Clark is a marketing major at the University of Iowa. In her sophomore year, the College

Sports Information Directors of America, now known as College Sports Communicators, named her a first-team Academic All-American (CSC). When Clark was a junior, the CSC named him the 2023 Academic All-American of the Year.

Conclusion

In "The Caitlin Clark Story: Inspiring Tales of an Unstoppable Rising Star," we are taken on a remarkable journey of perseverance, determination, and passion. Caitlin Clark's incredible story is a testament to the power of hard work and dedication in achieving one's dreams.

Through the pages of this book, we witness Caitlin's unwavering commitment to her craft and her unwavering spirit in the face of adversity. Her love for the game of basketball is palpable, and her unrelenting pursuit of excellence is truly inspiring.

As we read about Caitlin's rise to fame, we are reminded that success is not always easy, but with grit and determination, anything is possible. Her story is a beacon of hope for anyone who has ever faced obstacles in their pursuit of their goals.

In conclusion, "The Caitlin Clark Story" is a powerful and

uplifting read that will inspire readers of all ages to never give up on their dreams. Caitlin's journey is a reminder that with hard work, passion, and a never-give-up attitude, anything is possible. This book is a must-read for anyone looking for inspiration and motivation to chase their dreams and reach their full potential.